Everything You Need to Know About

BREAKING THE CYCLE OF DOMESTIC VIOLENCE

Living with the message that love is violent, you are at risk of becoming violent with the ones you love or choosing a violent partner.

Everything You Need to Know About

BREAKING THE CYCLE OF DOMESTIC VIOLENCE

Charlotte Kinstlinger-Bruhn

THE ROSEN PUBLISHING GROUP, INC.
NEW YORK

To my sons, Max Channing and Harrison Charles.
I know they will grow up to be gentle men.

The people pictured in this book are only models; they in no way practice or endorse the activities illustrated. Captions serve only to explain the subjects of the photographs and do not in any way imply a connection between the real-life models and the staged situations shown.

Published in 1997 by The Rosen Publishing Group, Inc.
29 East 21st Street, New York, NY 10010

First Edition
Copyright 1997 by The Rosen Publishing Group, Inc.

Manufactured in the United States of America.

Library of Congress Cataloging-in-Publication Data

Kinstlinger-Bruhn, Charlotte.
    Everything you need to know about breaking the cycle of domestic violence / Charlotte Kinstlinger-Bruhn. — 1st ed.
        p.   cm. — (The need to know library)
    Includes bibliographical references and index.
    Summary: Discusses domestic abuse, its warning signs, and healthy ways of dealing with it.
    ISBN 0-8239-2434-3
    1. Family violence—United States—Juvenile literature. 2. Family violence—Prevention—Juvenile literature. [1. Family violence.]
    I. Title. II. Series.
HQ809.3.U5K56 1997
362.82′92—dc21   97-10344
                                                        CIP
                                                         AC

Contents

Introduction

Kathy's father liked to take her camping, hiking, and to football games. He usually treated her well, but sometimes he insulted her and other times he hit her. She thought that the beatings were her fault and that maybe if she helped her mother more with the housework, he would stop.

As she became older, the beatings worsened. One night Kathy's father tried to strangle her with a telephone wire. A neighbor heard Kathy's screams and the police arrested her father.

Despite the way that her father treated Kathy, her mother wanted him home. She said that she needed him. After her father had spent a few nights in jail, Kathy's mother paid the bail money to have him released. Her father came home very upset. He cried when he told Kathy that he was sorry. He said that he would never hurt her again. He said that his own father had beat him, but he wanted to become a *better father. Kathy wanted to believe him, but she was still afraid.*

An act of domestic violence occurs every eighteen seconds in the United States. It can happen to anybody. Men, women, and children of all backgrounds are abused.

If one family or household member hits, hurts, or seriously threatens to hurt another family or household member, a serious crime has been committed. It is called domestic violence. And it can send the abuser to jail.

Domestic abuse is a pattern of controlling behavior. It can be physical, sexual, or emotional. Nobody has the right to hurt another person. Nobody deserves to be abused. You have a right to feel safe and to grow up without being hurt.

Many people believe violence is a learned behavior. If you see it in your family, you are more likely to continue it in your future relationships. Sixty percent of boys who witness violence in the home grow up to abuse their adult partners.

Victims of domestic violence are also three times more likely to be victimized again than are victims of other types of crime. This behavior is called the "cycle of violence." In this book you will learn how to recognize it, and how to break it.

If you have seen or experienced abuse in your life, you are not alone. One out of every three Americans has seen an incident of domestic

Domestic violence is controlling and forceful behavior that hurts
you.

violence. You have the right to expect protection. There are many organizations available to help you.

Whether or not you are the one being abused in your home, the experience of living with violence is terrifying and harmful. Abused people feel alone and are often ashamed of the abuse. They feel that they are to blame or that they deserve it. They may stay silent because they are afraid of being hurt by their abusers.

If you know someone who is being abused, it is important for you to talk to him or her. Show that you can be trusted. If you are the one being abused, find a good friend or a trusted adult. This is a brave and necessary step.

There are people who want to help you, but you need to reach out for the help. You need to make the decision to get out of the dangerous situation or the bad relationship. Your call will begin the healing process. It is the only way to break the cycle of domestic violence.

Putting your partner in fear through threats, actions, gestures, or a loud voice is emotional abuse.

Chapter 1

What Is Domestic Violence?

*M*ichael knew his friends beat their girl-friends. They talked—some even bragged—about it. Michael believed that physical violence was wrong. He treated his girlfriend, Ellen, like a queen. Many of her friends were jealous of how much he seemed to care. Michael and Ellen spent most of their time together. He took her out to movies and dinner; he paid for everything.

But he had another problem—he was jealous. At first Ellen was flattered. She liked the fact that he wanted to spend all of his time with her. But now he seemed to be getting worse. He was beginning to make her feel uncomfortable. He didn't like her talking to other guys, or going out alone with her girl-friends. She felt like he did not trust her.

One day, he surprised Ellen with tickets to see his favorite band. When she told him she had to study for an English exam, Michael became angry. He said she was wasting her time studying because she *was stupid. He threatened to go to the concert with another girl if she said no. Ellen changed her mind and went to the concert.*

Even though Michael did not hit Ellen, he is an abuser. By insulting her, threatening her, and cutting her off from her friends, he committed emotional abuse. Emotional abuse is also a form of domestic abuse.

People of every racial, ethnic, and economic group suffer from domestic abuse. A recent study conducted by the National Resource Center for Youth Services has shown that approximately one third of all high school and college relationships turn violent.

Abuse in relationships often happens to people who have less power and fewer ways to protect themselves: mainly women, children, and older adults. However, it is important to realize that women and children are not the only people mis-treated. Men can be abused by women, parents by their children, and teens by each other.

Domestic abuse is about a need for control. The abuser in a relationship will take complete control over the other person. The abuser will use the abuse to intimidate the victim. The abuser may also use abuse to deal with his or her own uncomfortable feelings. Hurting someone else is the method that the abuser has learned to deal with these feelings.

This is a destructive way for people to interact. No person should be in control of another. Healthy relationships are about equality and respect, not power and control.

The only way to stop abuse is to recognize what abuse is. Treating yourself and others with respect is a choice you make, no matter what situation you grew up in.

The Faces of Abuse

Abuse can be physical, emotional, or sexual. It is considered domestic violence if the person who harmed you is a family or household member. The law defines this as your spouse or former spouse; someone with whom you have a child in common; an adult person related to you by blood or marriage; an adult person who lives with you or used to live with you; someone with whom you have a legal parent/child relationship; or someone else who is at least sixteen years old who dates or has dated you in the past.

Physical Abuse. Physical abuse is violent or controlling physical contact that hurts you. It includes pushing, shoving, grabbing, scratching, hair-pulling, kicking, punching, or slapping. Twisting someone's arm until it causes pain, burning someone, or even extreme tickling are also forms of physical abuse.

Emotional Abuse. Emotional abuse is more difficult to see, but the effects are just as painful.

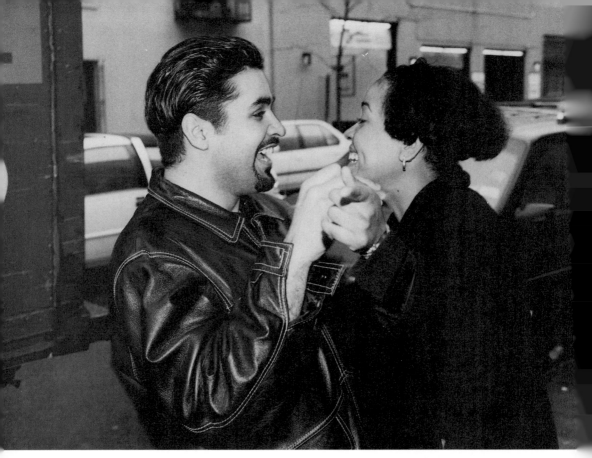

In a healthy relationship people respect each other. No one person has control.

Many people may not even realize they are being emotionally abused. Emotional abuse includes name-calling, insults, blaming, and threats.

Financial control (control through money) is also a form of emotional abuse. Perhaps the abuser keeps you from getting or keeping a job. Perhaps he or she makes you ask for money, or takes the money that you earn. Emotional abuse tears down your self-esteem. The abuser makes you feel worthless. He or she controls you and puts you down through words and threats instead of physical actions.

Emotional abuse is damaging and hurtful. It is just as important to seek counseling and safety for a victim of emotional abuse as it is for a victim of physical or sexual abuse.

Sexual Abuse. Sexual abuse is unwanted or forced sexual acts, demands, or insults. This includes verbal sexual harassment, unwanted touching, coerced sex, and rape. Sexual abuse can be committed by a stranger, family member, friend, or partner. According to a recent Massachusetts study, 60 percent of all rapes reported to rape crisis centers are committed by people who know the victims. The majority of the victims are aged sixteen to twenty-four.

What Is a Healthy Relationship?

Many teens confuse control with love. More than one in eight teenagers experience physical violence in their dating relationships. They think that when their boyfriend or girlfriend doesn't want them to have any other friends, it means he or she loves them too much to share them.

In a healthy relationship, men and women respect each other. Respect includes both the mind and the body. Love is *not* about control.

Love means trust and support. If your parents are in a healthy relationship, they trust and support each other—even if they do not always agree. In a healthy family, parents will trust and support you. In a healthy relationship, you can trust your

partner when he or she is talking to somebody
else. You understand that he or she has the right
to enjoy other friendships.

It is hard to know what a healthy relationship is
if you have never seen one in your house. Living
with the message that love is violent, you are at
risk of becoming violent with the ones you love,
or choosing a violent partner. Fifty-seven percent
of the teens who were abused as children had
been in a dating relationship in which violence
occurred. You have to learn how to make a
healthy relationship. A healthy relationship feels
good. It allows you to be the person you want
to be.

Chapter 2

The Cycle of Violence

*C*hico and Rochelle celebrated the anniversary
of their first date with dinner at a local restaurant.
When the waitress brought their food, Rochelle's
order was wrong. Even though Rochelle did not
care, Chico became angry. She tried to calm him
down, but he continued to make a scene. He yelled
at the waitress; then he yelled at Rochelle.

He told her that it was her fault. He said that she
had nagged him to go out. He said that she had
ruined his whole night, and that he was leaving.
Rochelle was left sitting alone.

After a few minutes she ran to the parking lot to
look for Chico's car. She was so glad to see him waiting for her that she told him she was sorry.

Rochelle did nothing wrong, but she felt the
need to apologize to Chico. No one deserves to be
insulted the way Chico insulted Rochelle. No one

In 1994, more than 1 million teens ran away from home. Most left to escape beating and sexual abuse at home.

deserves that type of embarrassment. Chico's behavior is abusive.

Even though the abuser will often feel ashamed of or guilty about the abuse, he or she will refuse to take responsibility for the actions. He or she may blame the victim for provoking the abuse, try and justify it, or deny it. This is wrong. Remember, the victim is never at fault when violence or abuse occurs. You may be vulnerable and needy, but nobody wants or deserves to be hurt.

It is important to remember that the problem is with the abuser. You cannot change an abuser. He or she must seek professional help. You do not have control over the violence in your house, or your partner's violence. You *do* have a choice about how to respond. You can break the cycle by getting yourself into a safe situation where you are treated with the respect that you deserve.

When Violence Is Familiar

An abuser has usually seen violence in his or her own family. Seventy-three percent of abusers were abused as children. An abuser never learned how to interact and establish a healthy relationship. Abused children grow up learning that it's okay to hurt other people or to let other people hurt them. In future relationships they will turn to the familiar method of interaction: violence. This is how a victim of domestic violence can turn into an abuser.

An abuser will create a pattern of behavior in his or her relationship. There will be good times and there will be bad times. The good times are often called the "honeymoon." These usually follow an episode of violence. During the honeymoon the abuser may seem very caring and sensitive. He or she will try and make up for the abuse, and per- haps even apologize for it. The worse the abuse is, the sweeter the honeymoon will be. Victims often stay in their relationships because they are waiting—and hoping—for the next good time. However, it is important to understand that abuse is a learned behavior. It is a "belief system," and only the abuser can change his or her behavior.

Warning Signs

Abusive behaviors are destructive and dangerous. In many cases they can be life- threatening. The dangers are real. An abuser could be your parent, sister, spouse, son, or yourself. While there is no stereotypical abuser, many abusers share similar qualities and act in similar ways.

Unreasonable anger, yelling, screaming, and insults can be warning signs of abuse. Extreme jealousy, control, and complaints are also danger signals that a situation is not healthy and could become violent.

Humiliation (Public and Private). An abuser does not think very highly of him or herself. He or

Insults can make a person feel hurt and worthless.

she feels better when insulting someone else. This is cruel and unhealthy behavior.

Jealousy. Extreme jealousy and possessiveness are not signs of true love. They are signs that the abuser sees you as an object to possess, not a person. An abuser feels that he or she "owns" you, like a new jacket.

Control. An abuser feels better when he or she is in total control. This is not healthy. When one person makes all the decisions, the other is left powerless and dependent on the abuser.

Watch for these and other clues, such as extreme anger, or a short temper. Trust your instincts if you think that you or someone else is in trouble.

The Cycle Continues

Being in an abusive situation is painful, but it is also familiar. Victims of abuse have not learned any other way to deal with feelings, problems, and people. A study of male batterers in Minnesota showed that 80 percent grew up in homes where they saw or suffered domestic abuse. Women who grew up in abusive homes were also more likely to find relationships where they hurt, or were being hurt by, someone else.

Other studies report the following:

- In at least half the instances where there is spousal abuse, there is also child abuse.
- Reports by battered mothers show that 87 percent of children witness the abuse.

Each person is responsible for his or her behavior. Even if you are very close to the abuser, the problem is with him or her. With professional help, it is possible that the abuser can learn to deal with people in a nonviolent and healthy way.

It's hard to say why someone you respect and trust would hurt you. There are no easy answers.

No Excuse

Whatever the excuse somebody has for being abusive, that doesn't mean it's okay. Jealousy, financial pressure, alcohol or drugs, depression, and other types of mental illness are the most common excuses given. An abuser may tell you that he or she had a bad day, or too much to drink. An abuser may tell you that you deserved to be hit because you are "stupid" or a "flirt."

These are just excuses. They are unacceptable. They are not true, and they are unfair. There is no excuse for abuse.

Chapter 3

How Domestic Violence Hurts You

*K*athy stopped trusting her father when he came home from jail. She didn't believe his apologies, and didn't believe that he could—or would—change. She started to hang around with an older crowd in her neighborhood. They encouraged her to stop going to class and to smoke marijuana and drink. Kathy started stealing alcohol from her father's liquor cabinet for her and her new friends. She hated her life at home. Her new friends understood this—they came from homes like hers.

One guy in the crowd started paying attention to Kathy. He was very good-looking and popular. She agreed to go to his house one day after school. His parents were not home.

He took her up to his bedroom and locked the door. They smoked a joint, and he started to kiss her. Kathy was scared. When Kathy told him she was scared, he laughed at her. He told her she was lucky

It takes time to get to know someone and decide if he or she is kind, healthy, and worthy of your good feelings.

that someone like him wanted her. Then he hit her. It was just like what her father had done to her. She had learned from her father that if she didn't want to get hit, she shouldn't fight. So she let him do whatever he wanted. Maybe this guy would really care about her if she didn't fight. Eventually she stopped caring about what happened to her.

When a partner makes you feel bad about yourself, it is hard to remember what it is like to feel good. If you grew up with parents who abused you, then an abusive situation might feel "normal" to you. But domestic violence can happen to anyone. Even if you came from a home where there

It takes more than expensive gifts to make someone a good partner.

was no abuse, an abusive partner can still pull you into his or her cycle of violence.

Everybody wants to be loved. When someone pays attention to you—a parent or a partner—it feels good. Maybe you think that the abuser has changed. He may compliment you. She may buy you things. The abuse rarely starts immediately. But when it does start, it will not stop.

Healthy relationships have conflicts too. While these conflicts can lead to arguments, in a healthy relationship no one person is in complete control. Problems are solved with discussion and under-standing, not with violence and insults.

Surviving the Abuse

Battering is the most common major injury to women; it occurs more frequently than car accidents, muggings, and rape combined. It is difficult to have an exact number because many victims are afraid to report the abuse and instead find ways to disguise it. Some invent stories about their injuries. Others deny it. Many abused people get family members, friends, teachers, even doctors to believe their stories. They may be ashamed to admit the abuse. They often feel trapped, alone, and scared.

Some people try to survive in their situations by isolating themselves from friends and family. They are afraid to trust anybody. This is a way of protecting themselves from more pain.

Victims will often think of their abuser as two people: the person who compliments them and the person who tells them that they are worthless. When you separate the abuser from the harm he or she causes, it becomes easier to focus on the good that he or she does. You try to forget the cruel side of him or her.

Staying in an abusive situation is dangerous. As a victim, you need to reach out for help. Find a trusted adult friend or family member who can help protect you. Explain the situation and express your feelings and fears. He or she will help you learn how to feel good and believe in yourself again, and support you when you are ready to get help.

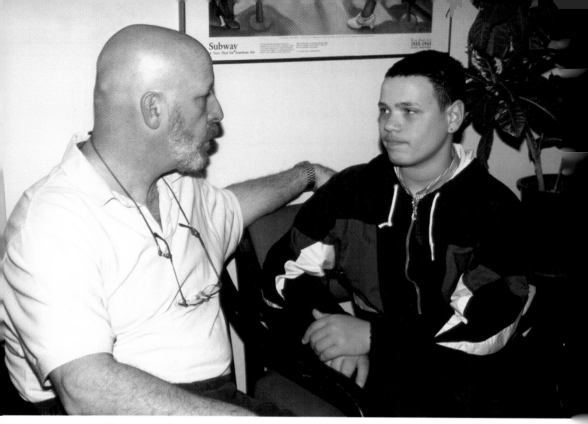

Talking with an adult friend or counselor can help you learn better ways to cope.

When you live with violence, either at home or in a dating relationship, drugs and alcohol may seem attractive. They appear to offer an escape from your nightmare. This is false. After the high wears off, your problems are still waiting for you.

You may feel like running away from home, dropping out of school, or dropping out of life. These are all normal feelings. When you are abused you lose your strength, hope, and self-respect. You may feel depressed and trapped. It may seem that there is no way out.

Some victims deal with their feelings by hurting others. This is how the cycle of violence continues.

Dropping out, running away, and doing drugs are only temporary escapes for your anger. They will not make your feelings of pain or depression go away; they will only make them worse.

The best way to stop the pain is to get out of the situation. While you cannot force the abuser to get help, you can get help for yourself. There is counseling available to help you deal with your emotions in a healthy way. But, before anyone can help you, you need to let people know that you are being abused. You need to ask for help.

How Can You Tell If a Friend Is Being Abused?

As you've already learned, victims of physical and sexual abuse often try to hide their injuries. They will go to great lengths to keep it a secret. However, there are some common warning signs.

- unexplained injuries
- mood changes; frequent periods of anger or silence
- requests for financial help

If you think your friend is being hurt, you may feel helpless. It is difficult to know what to say. You may feel awkward or uneasy about interfering in someone else's family or relationship, but abuse is everybody's business. Your friend's health and well-being are in danger because the abuse will not stop. It will only get worse.

ARE YOU A VICTIM OF DATING VIOLENCE?

- Are you frightened of your boyfriend or girlfriend's temper?
- Are you afraid to disagree with him or her?
- Do you find yourself apologizing to yourself or others for your boyfriend or girlfriend's behavior when you are treated badly?
- Have you been frightened by his or her violence towards others?
- Have you been hit, kicked, shoved or had things thrown at you?
- Do you not see friends or family because of his or her jealousy?
- Have you been forced to have sex?
- Have you been afraid to say no to sex?
- Are you forced to justify everything you do, every place you go and every person you see to avoid his or her temper?
- Have you been wrongly and repeatedly accused of flirting or having sex with others?
- Are you unable to go out, get a job or go to school without his or her permission?
- Have you become secretive, ashamed or hostile to your parents because of this relationship?

If a friend confides in you that he or she is being abused, there are many things you can do to help. Listening is the most important. Be sympathetic and careful not to blame or embarrass him or her. Encourage your friend to talk to a trusted adult—offer to go with her or him if necessary. Let her know that the abuse is the abuser's responsibility, not hers.

The most important thing is to make sure that she is safe. Work with her to plan her protection. If the situation becomes life-threatening, help your friend get to a safe place. There are many different organizations that provide help to victims of domestic violence. These include shelters, mental health centers, hospitals, private therapists, churches, temples, and social service organizations like the Salvation Army.

The "Community Services" section in the front of the White Pages of the phone book often lists local agencies that can help. You can also choose to call one of the hot lines provided in the Where to Go for Help list. Most offer 24-hour, toll free telephone service.

Do not be discouraged if she decides to stay in the relationship temporarily. Be patient with her and do not give up. It is often hard for someone to accept that she is in an abusive relationship—and even harder to get out of it. Remember that the love and support you give your friend may be the only love and support she has.

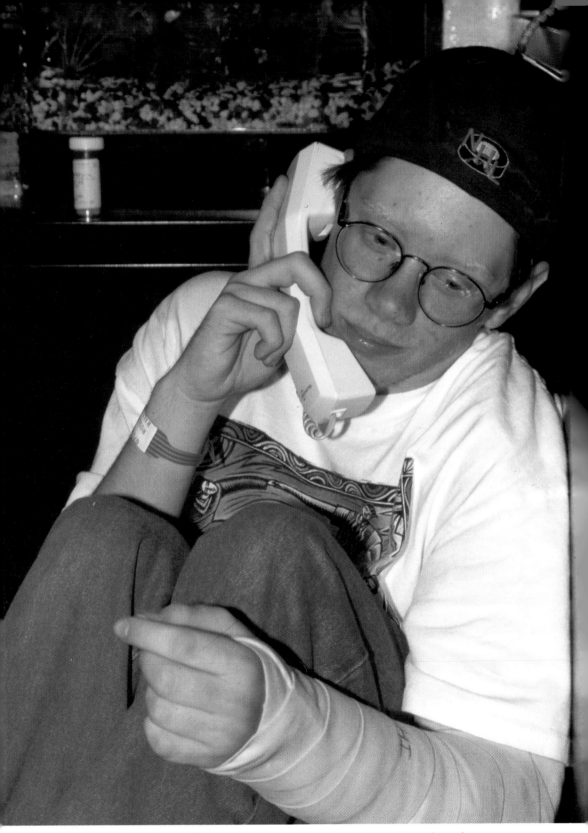

You are the one who will have to take action if you want the abuse
to stop. Calling for help is an important first step.

Trust Your Instinct

Abuse can come in many forms. Even though every situation is different, your instincts, or feelings, will tell you when something is wrong. It won't feel right. A "red flag" (warning sign) will rise when someone hits you or insults you.

When somebody crosses your boundary, listen to your interior warning signal. This is your personal security alarm. If a situation feels wrong, get out! No matter what the other person says to you, always trust your instinct. Only you can know what feels wrong, and only you can do something to change it.

If You Are Being Attacked

If you cannot get yourself out of an abusive situation, there are things you can do to protect yourself from injury.

If you sense an oncoming attack, try to be near a door to the outside or a door you can lock from the inside. Do not stand near an open window. Try to protect your face, chest, and abdomen from assault. Do not reason with your abuser or try to hit back. In most cases, the batterer will only become more angry. Do what you can to save yourself.

Create a code word that you can give to a trusted adult. If you need to call him or her for help, you can use this code word. It will signal that you are in trouble, but not alert the abuser.

If you can, call the police. In some states, the police can remove the abuser from the home on a temporary basis even if you do not press charges against him or her. This is called temporary protection. If the attack is serious, the police can make an arrest. They can also take you to a shelter (although most shelters will not take teenagers without a guardian), or to the home of a trusted adult. They will help you receive medical treatment and provide you with helpful information on your legal rights.

If you receive medical help, ask the doctor or nurse to take pictures of your injuries. These photographs can be used later as evidence if you decide you want court protection. Save torn clothing, and broken or damaged objects—anything that can be used to show evidence of abuse.

Domestic violence does not go away on its own. You will have to take action if you want the abuse to stop. Remember, domestic violence is a crime, and you do not have to tolerate it. You have the right to live a healthy, successful life.

Chapter 4

Know Your Rights and Recourse

D omestic abuse is against the law in most states when it causes or threatens physical or sexual violence. But the law—and how it will apply to you as the victim of domestic violence—differs from state to state. Even the definition of a domestic relationship varies from state to state. Many advocate groups are trying to establish laws that would recognize emotional abuse as a crime punishable by law. As of now, they do not exist.

Every state has two sets of laws: criminal and civil. Under the criminal laws in most states, physical and sexual abuse, or threat of this kind of abuse, is a crime. The abuser has broken a law and can be tried, and punished, as a criminal.

Cases of domestic violence under civil law are handled in family court. In family court the abuse is not looked at as a crime. It is looked at as a violation of your rights as a private citizen. It is important to remember that the laws will differ for different types of relationships (i.e. parent/child, girlfriend/boyfriend).

No matter what your relationship is to your abuser, you have rights as a victim of violence. You have the right to expect help and protection. You can achieve this protection through either the criminal or the civil court.

Criminal. If you would like to press criminal charges against the abuser, you can call the police and report him or her. The police will then write up a report of the abuse. A written report is required by law. Be sure to insist that it is in fact written down.

If your abuser is arrested for or charged with a crime you have the right to ask the police to obtain a "No Contact Order." This prevents the abuser from having any contact with you.

Civil. If you do not want to press criminal charges but you do want to protect yourself, you can request an order of protection. This sets limits on the behavior of the abuser. He or she will no longer be able to threaten or hurt you. If he or she breaks this order, the courts will punish him or her.

Abuse in the Home

If you are being physically or sexually abused by one of your parents, your rights as a minor (under the age of eighteen) are complicated.

In most states when you tell any adult—a school official, a doctor, a nurse, a therapist, a police officer, or a domestic violence advocate—that you are being abused, they are considered mandated reporters. They are required by law to report the abuse to the child protective services in your area. If you do not want to report your abuse then you can call a domestic violence agency and ask for help anonymously. Most advocates will answer your questions even if you do not want to give your name.

The child protective agency in your state will open an investigation once the abuse has been reported. They will interview you, your parents, and anyone else involved in the situation. During the investigation, the child protective agency may decide that it is necessary that you live outside the home. This is for your own safety. You will be asked to stay with a trusted adult or family member.

An order of protection may also take custody away from the abusive parent and allow him or her only supervised visits with you. The supervision can be provided by the other parent, a social worker, or a trusted adult friend.

In most cases the abusive parent can no longer live in the same place as you. He or she must leave your home, or arrange to have you stay with a guardian. If both parents are abusive, the court may place you in a foster home.

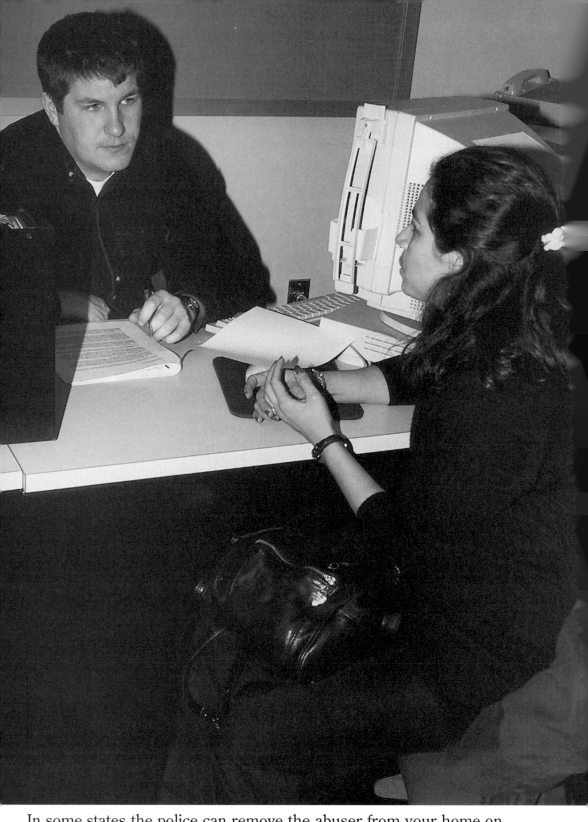

In some states the police can remove the abuser from your home on a temporary basis, even if you do not press charges. If the attack is serious, the police can usually make an arrest.

You can also ask the court for emancipation. This means the court considers you to be an adult and allows you to live on your own. For this to happen, most states require that you be over sixteen years old.

Violence in Dating Relationships

If you and the abuser are dating and you are both over sixteen years old, most courts will recognize yours as a "domestic relationship"—even if you have never lived together.

Physical and sexual abuse is a crime. Criminal charges can be brought against your partner, such as assault, harassment, or rape.

There are other types of restraining orders you can receive against the abuser if you do not qualify for an order of protection. Each state will provide you with different options.

When Abuse Is Emotional

Emotional abuse is not yet considered a crime. Though many laws are being discussed, right now the states have a very narrow definition of domestic violence. However, emotional abuse is still extremely destructive. You have a right to seek help and relief.

Domestic violence agencies will help you answer questions about your relationship. They will offer suggestions to help you find a way out of the

Attorneys can help abuse victims learn their legal rights.

emotional abuse. Many domestic violence agencies also offer support groups. Some of these groups are aimed at teenagers like you. Many of the organizations listed in the Where to Go for Help section can provide you with support groups in your area.

Do You Have a Right to an Attorney?

If your abuse case goes to criminal court, your rights are represented by a prosecutor who will prosecute the crime (the physical or sexual violence).

In civil court (family court), a guardian may be required to act in your best interests. The civil court also will appoint a lawyer to represent you free of charge.

In most states you can pursue your case in both criminal and civil court. It depends on your needs and goals. You might want to go to civil court while also seeking relief from the abuse through the criminal courts with an order of protection. You might ask to be removed from your home— though the choice ultimately will be made by the family court judge.

Many states have a crime victims agency that can offer you assistance. They will answer your legal questions and work with you and your family to understand your rights. In other states a domestic violence advocate will help you to file orders, accompany you in court, and answer your legal questions.

You have the choice to press charges against the abuser. You may decide to leave the abuser and seek help. But if your life is in danger, you need to get out of the situation for good. The abuse will not stop unless the situation is changed.

Chapter 5

Breaking the Cycle

*K*athy *moved out of her house to live with her boyfriend and his family. Soon she realized her life was just as bad as it had been at home. Her boyfriend beat and sexually abused her, and his parents fought often.*

Kathy had a math teacher whom she felt she could trust. This teacher had once told Kathy to call her at home if Kathy ever needed to talk. Kathy had saved that number, and now decided to call. She was afraid that something terrible would happen to her if she didn't.

Kathy and her teacher met for coffee. Her teacher gave her the number of an organization that worked with victims of domestic violence. She tried to make Kathy understand the danger of the situation. "Make a good plan," the teacher told Kathy, "and be sure that you have a safe place to go once you leave. The

If you need to get out of a dangerous situation, you should tell someone who can help you.

counselor at the organization I gave you will help you see that none of this is your fault."

Although it is normal to feel alone, reaching out for help is the beginning of the healing process.

The first step is to tell someone you trust, a close friend or a trusted relative, about the abuse. If you feel you cannot tell a parent, tell another adult—a teacher, doctor, or friend's parent. Remember that when you tell an adult, in many cases they are required to report the abuse to the child protective services in your area. Telling

People who are abusers can change, but they have a
serious problem and need to seek help from a counselor or
other professional.

someone is the first step to getting out of the
situation.

Healing is a journey. It starts with a question:
"What can I do?" There are many different answers. Ultimately, the choice is up to you. You
need to make the choice that will help you become
a happier, healthier person.

Leaving an Abusive Dating Relationship

People who abuse others are afraid to lose control. While leaving the abuser is often the best

Chapter 6
Looking Ahead

*R*ochelle was tired of feeling bad about herself whenever she was with Chico. She broke up with him and started hanging out with her girlfriends again. They said they missed her. Truth is, she missed them too. She had a lot more fun with people who treated her well. Her friends didn't say, "Thought you were on a diet?" when they went out for ice cream. Those were the kinds of things Chico would say. And when she would get mad at him, he would says things such as, "I care about you. Nobody else tells you the truth."

Slowly Rochelle began to understand the difference between love and abuse. It hurt her sometimes to remember how badly Chico had treated her. She wondered how a smart girl like her could be so dumb when it came to picking partners, but now she knew the difference. She was never going to choose someone like Chico again.

This can be a good time to go out and make new friends, and to be around people who are good to you and who believe that you are a good person.

Though it was difficult, Rochelle broke the cycle and got back her life and her self-esteem. You can too. It is important that you remember it's not your fault!

As a victim of domestic violence, you do not have to suffer in silence. Reach out to an adult you trust for help. In some cases your situation may be too dangerous for you to seek help. In this case, your first priority is to get yourself out of the situation immediately.

Building a new life takes time. Many states have support groups for teenagers who are being

abused. Talking to other teens about your experience will make you feel less alone. Their stories
will be familiar to you, and yours will be to them.
You can bring the things you have learned about
your relationship to others. These meetings can
give you a safe opportunity to explore your feelings. You can bring your questions and your
fears. You will not be judged, and you will get
information.

Once you are safe, it is important to feel good
about yourself again. You are a valuable person.
You will need to teach yourself new ways of form-
ing a relationship. You will need to learn new ways
to deal with people. Increasing your independence
is an important first step.

The more independent you are, the better your
chance at breaking the cycle of abuse and moving
on with your life. You need to know that you are a
responsible, intelligent person. You need to know
that you can take care of yourself. It is okay to
look to others for support and love, but you
need to respect yourself and know that you are
strong. Here are some ways to increase your
independence:

- Learn the public transportation routes near
  your home. Knowing these routes allows you
  your own mode of transportation.
- Find ways to get yourself to and from appoint-
  ments, school, and work.

Getting a part-time job is a good way to begin gaining independence.

- Learn the names and numbers of a trusted adult, doctor, social worker, and your landlord. Record these and other important numbers in your own address book.
- Get a part-time job so that you can earn your own money.
- If possible, open your own bank account and learn how it works.

These steps are not easy. It will take time to learn how good emotional health feels. But take the time—it is worth it. Being with people who support you, value you, and respect you is something you deserve.

You cannot change the batterer, but you can change yourself. By regaining control of your life and learning to respect and love yourself as an individual, you can break the cycle of domestic violence.

Appendix

Personalized Safety Plan

Here is a personalized safety plan. These steps represent a plan to increase your safety and to help you prepare in advance for the possibility of future violence. Please fill in your answers on a separate sheet of paper.

Step 1. Safety during a violent incident.
I can use some or all of the following strategies:

A. If I decide to leave, I will _____.
(Practice how to get out safely. What doors, windows, elevators, stairwells, or fire escapes would you use?)

B. I can keep my purse or my wallet and car keys ready and put them _____ in order to leave quickly.

C. I can tell _____ about the violence and request that he/she call the police if suspicious noises are heard from my house. In case an emergency happens when he/she is not available,

I can also tell _____ about the violence.

D. I will use _____ as my code word with my children or friends so they can call for help when I say the code word.

E. If I have to leave my home, I will go _____. (Decide this even if you don't think there will be a next time.) If I cannot go to the location above, then I can go to _____ or _____.

F. When I expect we are going to have an argument, I will try to move to a space that is the lowest risk, such as _____. (Try to avoid arguments in the bathroom, garage, kitchen, near weapons or in rooms without access to an outside door.)

G. I will use my judgment and intuition. If the situation is very serious, I can give my parent or my partner what he/she wants to calm him/her down. I have to protect myself until I am out of danger.

Step 2. Safety when preparing to leave.
Leaving must be done with a careful plan so as to increase your safety. Batterers often strike back when they believe that the person they are battering is trying to leave the relationship/family.

I can use some or all of these safety strategies:

A. I will leave money and an extra set of keys with _____ so I can leave quickly.

B. I will keep copies of important documents or keys at _____.

C. I will open a savings account by _____, to increase my independence.

D. Other things I can do to increase my independence include: _____.

E. The domestic violence program hotline number is _____. I can seek shelter by calling this hotline.

F. I can keep change for phone calls on me at all times. To keep my telephone communications confidential, I must either use coins or get a friend to permit me to use his or her telephone credit card for a limited time when I first leave.

G. I will check with _____ and _____ to see who would be able to let me stay with them or lend me some money.

H. I can leave extra clothes with _____.

I. I will sit down and review my safety plan every _____ to plan the safest way to leave the residence. _____ (domestic violence advocate or friend) has agreed to help me review this plan.

Step 3. Safety and my emotional health.
The experience of being battered and verbally degraded is tiring and emotionally draining. Building a new life for myself takes much courage and energy. I can do some of the following:

A. If I feel down and ready to return to a potentially abusive situation, I can _____.

B. When I have to talk to the person who has abused me in person or by telephone, I can _____.

C. I can try to use "I can . . . " statements with myself and to be assertive with others.

D. I can tell myself—"_____"— whenever I feel others are trying to control or abuse me.

E. I can read _____ to help me feel stronger.

F. I can call _____, _____ as other resources to be of support to me.

G. Other things I can do to help me feel stronger are _____, _____, and _____.

H. I can attend workshops and support groups at the domestic violence program, or _____, and _____ to gain support and strengthen my relationships with other people.

Step 4. Items to take when leaving.
When you are leaving your home it is important to take some items with you. You might put these items in one place, so that if you have to leave in a hurry you can grab them quickly.

When I leave I should take: (you may not have some these items, or have access to them)
identification for myself
my birth certificate
my Social Security card
school and vaccination records
money
checkbook, ATM (Automatic Teller Machine) card
credit cards
keys—house/car
driver's license and registration
medications
work permit
green card
passport

medical records
pictures
jewelry
items of special sentimental value

Telephone numbers I need to know:

Police department _____
Battered women's program _____
County registry of protection orders _____
Minister or Rabbi _____
Other _____

Glossary—*Explaining New Words*

advocate   Someone who supports you and speaks on your behalf in court.

anonymous   By or from a person whose name is not known or given.

batterer   Someone who batters or beats another person.

civil law   The law of your rights as a private citizen.

coerce   To cause an event or action through force.

criminal law   The law of crimes and their punishments.

custody   The keeping and care of a person or thing.

demean   To make someone feel bad and inferior.

emancipation   The release of someone from a type of control, like a teen being legally treated as an adult, not a child.

emotional abuse   Cruel and controlling behavior, usually through insults, threats, and financial control.

evidence Facts or proof that an action or event occurred.

financial control Control of someone through money.

investigation A search or close examination.

learned behavior Behavior that someone has learned from watching or experiencing.

mandated reporter Any adult (in most states) required to tell child protective services about the abuse of a minor.

order of protection An enforceable civil court order that will direct the abuser to keep away from the victim of abuse.

physical abuse Violent or controlling physical contact that hurts you; includes hitting, pushing, shoving, pinching, and burning.

prosecutor The lawyer who tries to convict someone of unlawful behavior.

self-esteem Confidence, value, and happiness with yourself.

sexual abuse Unwanted or forced sexual acts, demands, or insults; including sexual insults, unwanted touching, and rape.

stereotypical One idea or behavior that many people believe is typical and normal.

Where to Go for Help

The "Community Services" section in the front of the White Pages in the phone book often lists local agencies helping victims of domestic violence. Most of the hotlines listed below offer 24-hour, toll free telephone service to victims of domestic violence.

Battered Women's Justice Project
(800) 903-0111 (hot line)

Domestic Abuse
(800) 799-SAFE (hot line)

Emerge: A Men's Counseling Service on Domestic
   Violence
18 Hurley Street, Suite 100
Cambridge, MA 02141
(617) 422-1550

Impact Personal Safety
(800) 345-5425

National Coalition Against Domestic Violence
P.O. Box 18749
Denver, CO 80218-0749
(303) 839-1852

National Council on Child Abuse and Family Violence
(800) 222-2000 (hot line)

National Network to End Domestic Violence
701 Pennsylvania Avenue N.W., Suite 900
Washington, DC 20004
(202) 434-7405
(800) 903-0111 ext. 3 (hot line)

National Runaway Switchboard
(800) 621-4000

Parents Anonymous
(800) 421-0353 (24 hour hot line)

For Further Reading

Acquaintance/Date Rape Information Sheet.
Wisconsin Coalition Against Sexual Assault,
1992.

Dating Violence: The Hidden Secret. Seattle, WA:
Intermedia, Inc., 1993.

Ingrassia, Michele, and Melinda Beck. "Patterns of
Abuse." *Newsweek* (July 4, 1994): pp. 26–33.

Levy, Barrie. *In Love and In Danger.* Seattle, WA:
Seal Press, 1993.

Nicarthy, Ginny. *Getting Free: A Handbook for
Women in Abusive Relationships.* Seattle, WA:
Seal Press, 1984.

Rue, Nancy. *Everything You Need to Know About
Abusive Relationships.* New York: The Rosen
Publishing Group, 1996.

Worchester, Nancy. "A More Hidden Crime:
Adolescent Battered Women." *Women's
Health: Readings on Social, Economic and
Political Issues.* Dubuque, IA: Kendall/Hunt
Publishing, 1993.

Index

M
minors, rights of, 36–37, 39

N
National Resource Center for
     Youth Services, 12
No Contact Order, 36

P
physical abuse
    definition of, 13
    escapes from, 28–29
    laws against, 35, 39
    seeking help from, 27, 43–46,
        48–51
    surviving the, 27
pressing charges, 36, 41
protection
    of a friend, 31
    order of, 37, 39, 41
    self, 33
    temporary, 34

R
rape, 15, 39
relationships, 13, 15, 17, 26, 36
restraining order, 39
rights of victim, 36–39

S
safety, of a friend, 31
safety plan, personalized, 52–
     57
self-esteem, 14, 48
shame, 9, 27, 30
support groups, 39–40, 48–49

T
trust, 15

W
warning signs
    of abuse, 29
    of an abuser, 20–22

Acknowledgments
Page 30, "Questions to Ask Yourself," © 1991 by Barrie Levy. Reprinted
from *In Love and In Danger: A Teen's Guide to Breaking Free of
Abusive Relationships*. Published by Seal Press, Seattle. A special
acknowledgment to the City Attorney's Office, San Diego, Calif., for
permission to reprint excerpts from the pamphlet "Teens in a Violent
Dating Relationship;" and to the Mental Health Association of
Westchester, White Plains, New York, for their invaluable research
materials and assistance.

About the Author
Charlotte Kinstlinger-Bruhn has been a professional writer for more
than nine years. She has won several awards from the New York Press
Association and has reported on numerous subjects including domestic
violence. She lives with her two sons, Max and Harrison, in Phoenicia,
New York.

Photo Credits
Cover photo by Michael Brandt; photograph on page 18 by Seth
Dinnerman; all other photos by Ira Fox.